WALKS IN TH
OF NORF

Giant hogweed rears its ugly head on the marshy bank of the Broad by the University of East Anglia.

Josie Briggs

With illustrations by the author

S.B. Publications

For my husband, Andrew

First published in 1998 by S. B. Publications,
c/o 19 Grove Road, Seaford, East Sussex BN25 1TP

ISBN 1 85770 165 8

Designed and typeset by CGB, Lewes
Printed by MFP Design and Print
Longford Trading Estate, Thomas Street,
Stretford, Manchester M32 0JT

CONTENTS

Front cover: View from Stone Hill, Beeston Regis Heath, looking towards
Beeston Bump.
Back cover: Thompson Common.

ACKNOWLEDGEMENTS

I would like to thank the following for their help and information:
Norfolk Wildlife Trust (Foxley Wood, Thompson Common, East
Wretham Heath); David Bingham, Royal Society for the Protection of
Birds (Snettisham); John Davies, Broads Authority (South Walsham
Broad); John Hovey, head groundsman of the University of East Anglia
(The university and Yare Valley); and Huby Fairhead, Norfolk and
Suffolk Aviation Museum, Flixton (history of East Wretham Heath).

I am especially grateful to my husband, Andrew, for his help in route
planning, proof reading and keeping me on the right tracks in the wilds
of Norfolk.

ABOUT THE AUTHOR

Josie Briggs has lived in Norfolk since 1988 and has explored much of its
countryside with its various wildlife habitats. She is interested in conservation and organic gardening and has contributed articles to several
publications, including *Organic Gardening, Suffolk and Norfolk Life,
Country Gardens and Smallholdings, Amateur Gardening*, and the
Countryman.
Josie is also a tutor in chemistry and other sciences.

INTRODUCTION

WILD places are not necessarily isolated places. Some of the sites featured in this book are near, even within, town and city boundaries. The common link is that all are managed in ways that are sympathetic to wildlife preservation.

The walks described are wholly or partly in nature reserves and conservation areas throughout Norfolk. Some are near the coast, overlooking mudflats, saltmarshes and beaches important for migrating birds and rare wildflowers. Others pass among the pine woods and heaths of Breckland, or along the dikes and rivers of Broadland, or into secret havens at the edges of towns.

Although it was intended to plan circular walks, with a couple of the long narrow sites along river banks or sea shore this proved impossible, but all of the walks have at least some circular element. Of course, these routes can be modified to make them shorter or, in some cases, longer. The nature reserves and conservation sites are worth exploring for their own sake, not just as part of a walk, and should appeal both to ramblers and nature lovers. Information on the history and wildlife of the area is given for each walk.

Most of the walks should take about half a day, and stopping places for picnics are indicated. To make a complete day out, nearby places of interest are given. Being a holiday region, Norfolk includes many attractions and amusements, catering for all interests and ages. There is a list of some of them at the end of the book.

Visitors to nature reserves are generally requested to keep to marked paths and trails to avoid damaging habitats. Dogs must be kept under control in nature reserves (in some, dogs are not allowed at all) and when passing through fields containing livestock. Information about the state of the paths, and any difficulties such as stiles or sand dunes, is given in each section.

The county of Norfolk contains a fantastic variety of countryside within

Sheep graze at East Wretham on areas of grass heathland reclaimed centuries ago from dense forest.

its borders, shaped by a long and varied history. Around 10,000 years ago, the melting ice sheets from the last Ice Age left undulating low hills of moraine in the north, known as the Cromer-Holt Ridge. Further south the land is flatter with gentle river valleys. Soft cliffs are eroding away along parts of the coast while other regions are growing outwards, forming sand spits, saltmarshes and mudflats.

Mankind's activities over the centuries have actually encouraged wildlife by creating new habitats. Originally covered with dense forest, parts of the county were cleared for farming and settlements. This gave rise to large areas of grass heathland, kept clear by grazing animals. Large scale peat excavations in the east flooded and became the Norfolk Broads. Fens have been drained to provide grazing land with clear water dikes and ditches.

All these habitats, natural and artificial, supported their own wildlife and developed their own ecosystems. It is only during this century that population growth, intensive agriculture, conifer plantations, pollution, and spreading towns and roads have taken their toll on the countryside.

Many of the woods, heaths, hedgerows, meadows and marshes were lost.

Fortunately, large areas have been acquired by conservation organisations and concerned individuals and are being managed as wildlife havens. Owners of nature reserves, Sites of Special Scientific Interest and other conservation areas include Norfolk Wildlife Trust, the National Trust, and the Royal Society for Protection of Birds. Numerous smaller sites – common ground or privately owned – are managed as wildlife havens by local councils and their owners, and many of these are open to the public. The Countryside Commission, the Council for Protection of Rural England, the Broads Authority and Norfolk County Council provide advice and financial support for many of these sites, and local volunteers provide much of the labour.

There has been an encouraging trend recently towards conservation and more sensitive management of the countryside in general, fuelled by increasing public concern and awareness of habitat loss and pollution. New hedgerows and tree belts are being planted along road sides. Verges and village greens are being left uncut for much of the year, and there are more wildflowers now than there were even a few years ago.

Nevertheless, the nature reserves and conservation sites will continue to play a pivotal role in preserving Norfolk's countryside. It is hoped that this book will encourage you to explore some of these wilder places, enjoying this county's unique and beautiful scenery and the wildlife which lives here.

Josie Briggs

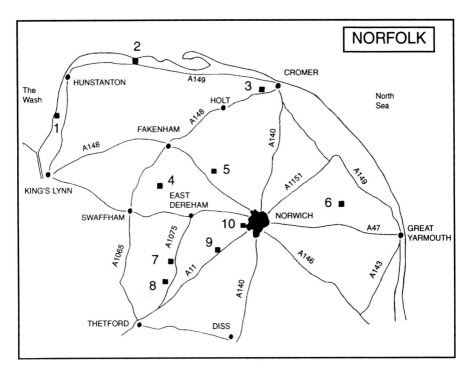

LOCATION OF WALKS

1 Snettisham Nature Reserve
2 Holkham Bay Nature Reserve
3 Roman Camp and Beeston Regis Heath
4 Litcham Common and the Nar Valley
5 Foxley Wood Nature Reserve
6 South Walsham Broad and the River Bure
7 Thompson Common Nature Reserve
8 East Wretham Heath Nature Reserve
9 Tiffey Valley, Wymondham
10 University of East Anglia and the Yare Valley

KEY TO MAPS

1 Maps are drawn to scale.

2 Numbers on maps are points of interest referred to in the text.

3 P denotes car parking.

4 Dotted lines denote boundaries of woods.

5 Other symbols as on Ordnance Survey maps.

THE WALKERS' CODE

1 Keep to marked paths and trails.

2 Fasten gates behind you.

3 Keep dogs under control (dogs are not allowed in some nature reserves).

4 Do not drop litter.

5 Do not disturb wildlife or livestock.

6 Do not pick or dig up any plants.

7 On roads without footpaths, keep to the right facing oncoming traffic.

8 Obey any rules specific to a site (see display boards at entrances to reserves).

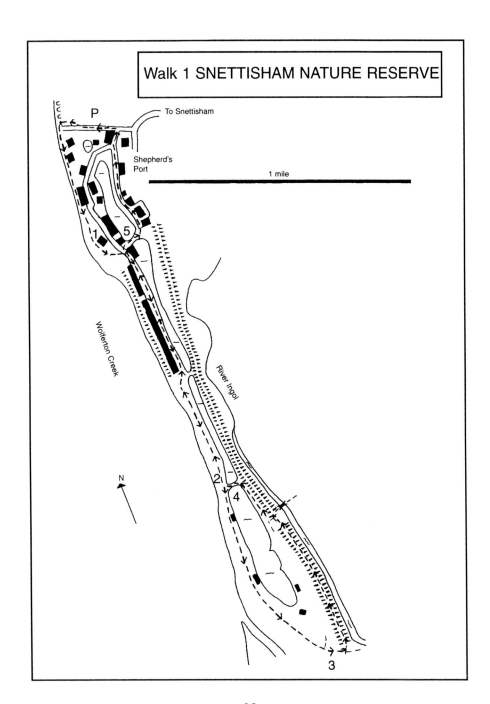

Walk 1 SNETTISHAM NATURE RESERVE

P

To Snettisham

Shepherd's
Port

1 mile

Wolferton Creek

River Ingol

N

1
5
2
4
3

Walk 1

SNETTISHAM NATURE RESERVE

Distance   Five miles

Map   OS Landranger 132

Start/Parking Snettisham Beach car park at Shepherd's Port; grid ref.
TF648336. In summer there is a small fee for the use of
this car park.

Nearest town Snettisham

THIS walk should appeal not only to bird watchers and nature lovers,
but to everyone who enjoys fine and varied scenery. The Royal Society
for the Protection of Birds' reserve covers 1,300 hectares on the banks of
the Wash, Britain's largest estuary, and is dominated by a chain of coastal
lagoons known as pits.

These saltwater pools, together with mud flats, salt marshes and shingle
beach, make this area an important site for migratory birds and in autumn
and winter large flocks of waders may be seen feeding on the mudflats.
The reserve is also colourful in summer with wildflowers, some rare.
There are good views over the Wash, coastline and inland countryside.

The reserve is open at all times. Dogs should be kept under close
control and visitors are asked to respect the privacy of chalet owners.
Paths are generally good, except for the one on the top of the river
embankment, which is narrow and overgrown in places. The lower
alternative path is in better condition but misses out on the excellent
view.

There are public lavatories on the beach near the start of the walk,
also a cafe – but it is not always open. An RSPB visitor centre is near
the car park. Visitors with disabilities may, after contacting the warden,
drive as far as the first hide.

11

Route directions

FROM the car park, head towards the estuary and climb the steps. From here there is a clear view over the mud flats ahead. Heacham is visible on the coast to the north, and King's Lynn to the south.

Turn left along the embankment. On both sides of the path there is a tapestry of wildflowers growing in the shingle in summer. The lagoons are visible behind the caravans on the left, with attractive undulating wooded countryside beyond. Just after passing the cafe on the left (1), descend on to the concrete track following the lakeside. The estuary embankment to the right is private – for chalet owners only. Water birds can be seen here, and in summer there is an amazing variety of flowers growing in the sandy soil along the bank, including some garden escapees such as ornamental poppies in various colours. Continue through the gate and climb up towards the embankment on the right,

A profusion of wild flowers – the bright yellow of ragwort, the purply grey of the teazel – on the west bank of the lake.

leaving the chalets behind and entering uninhabited countryside. At the south end of the third lagoon there are some benches (2) and this is a convenient place for a picnic.

Continue along the path which now runs along the bank of the fourth and final lagoon. There are several bird watchers' hides overlooking this water, but the waterside itself is fenced off to protect the waterfowl. Towards the south end of this lagoon an embankment blocks the water from sight, but there is a good view of the estuary and surrounding countryside. The mud flats change to salt marsh in this region.

At the gap in the fence (3), ignore the marker post to the left which marks the lower alternative path, and continue ahead on the narrow path and climb up on to the embankment. From here there are excellent views of the countryside to the right, with Snettisham church in the distance to the northeast. The salt marshes, lagoons and estuary spread out on the left.

Continue northwards along the embankment path. Below on the right, runs the River Ingol with reeds along its banks and lush wetland wildflowers in the low lying meadows. On reaching a barbed wire fence across the embankment, descend and turn right. The path follows the waterside, then turns left and crosses the land bridge (4) between the third and fourth lagoons. This is a good vantage point for looking over the water with its diversity of wildfowl. One of the easiest to spot is the oystercatcher with its long bright orange bill, smart black and white plumage and pink legs.

The oystercatcher

At the other side, turn right and retrace the original trail. At the gate across the track by the chalets, take the lower path and walk back along the lakeside. Take the clear path on the right leading between the chalets to the land bridge between the first and second lagoons (5). Here there is another good view of the water. At the other side, turn left, follow the lakeside road, turn right towards the shop and then left back to the car park.

The view across the salt water lagoons where in winter the sky is alive with tens of thousands of visiting geese and huge flocks of wading birds.

History and Wildlife

THE Wash is the most important British estuary for wintering and migrating birds and is a Grade I Site of Special Scientific Interest. It provides winter feeding and roosting sites for hundreds of thousands of wading birds and wildfowl, providing spectacular sights particularly during high tides in autumn and winter.

Snettisham Nature Reserve was acquired by the RSPB in 1973. Its mud flats, salt marsh, shingle beach and coastal lagoons are all important wildlife habitats. In summer, ringed plovers and oyster catchers roost on the beach. There is a breeding colony of terns on islands in the lagoons. Other birds include pink-footed geese, sedge and reed warblers, redshank, plovers and nightjars. At certain times of year, tremendous flocks of migrant birds make a spectacular display as they stop off here to feed on the plentiful supply of lugworms, cockles, winkles and other creatures buried in the mud.

Knots are the most numerous of the wading birds at Snettisham, with around 32,000 spending winter here. Other waders include large flocks of oystercatchers and dunlins.

The shingle beach supports a surprising variety of flowers from May throughout summer. These include yellow horned poppies, vipers bugloss, sea holly, sea pea, sea campion, ragwort and various thistles. Lagoon side plants include sea buckthorn, senecio, teasel and mallow.

Places of Interest

SNETTISHAM has a church with a lofty spire and a fine west front and the attractive eighteenth century Dutch-gabled Old Hall. However, its greatest claim to fame is the discovery there, in 1948 of a treasure hoard of Iron Age torcs, or collars, now in Norwich Castle Museum.

The yellow horned poppy.

At nearby Heacham the picturesque Caley Mill stands among the lavender fields which produce a crop made into lavender water and other scented products. Admission is free to Northern Lavender which has demonstration gardens, a plant centre, gift shop and tea room but there is a charge for a guided tour of the lavender distilleries.

Sandringham House has been a favourite home of the royal family since Edward VII bought it in 1861, when he was Prince of Wales. It is the Queen's private property but when the royals are not in residence the gardens are open to the public and many excellent picnic sites have been provided on the estate which has variety of scenery including farmland, heath, woodland and salt marshes About five miles north of Snettisham is Hunstanton, the largest seaside resort in West Norfolk. It has a sandy beach backed by cliffs formed of alternate layers of white and red chalk and red carstone.

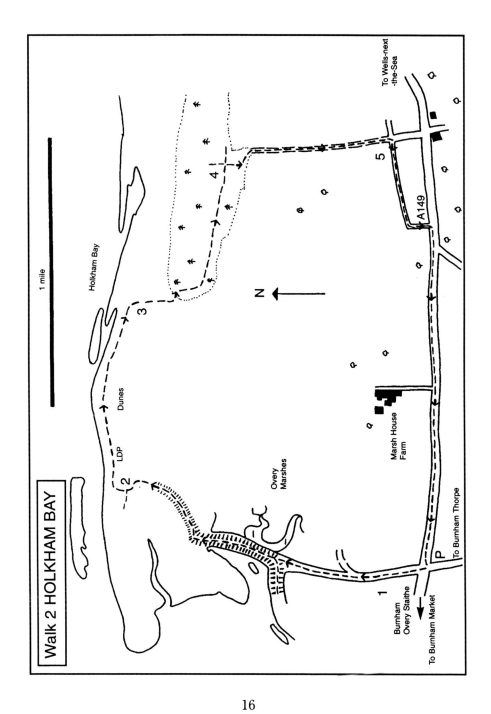

Walk 2 HOLKHAM BAY

1 mile

Holkham Bay

Dunes

LDP

Overy Marshes

N

Marsh House Farm

Burnham Overy Staithe

To Burnham Market

To Burnham Thorpe

To Wells-next -the-Sea

A149

P

1 2 3 4 5

HOLKHAM BAY NATURE RESERVE

Distance   Six miles

Map   OS Landranger 132

Start/Parking   The layby at the junction of the A149 with the road to Burnham Thorpe; grid ref. TF853439

Nearest town   Wells-next-the Sea

MOST of this walk passes through the magnificent Holkham National Nature Reserve on the north Norfolk coast. This large reserve contains a variety of fine scenery and habitats and is important for migratory and breeding birds. Its saltmarsh wildflowers are spectacular in summer.

Starting at Overy Marshes, the trail joins the Peddars Way and Norfolk Coastal Path before turning inland again. In order to make this walk circular, the final stage is along the verge of the A149 but, if preferred, the walk could be done as an 'out and return' as far as the pine wood.

The path is hard going in places, particularly along the beach and among the sand dunes, and care should be taken at high tide or in rough weather. Dogs must be kept under control. Cycling is not allowed on the dunes.

Route directions

CROSS the road and go through the metal gate and along the public footpath towards the shore. Hedges tower on both sides at first, and the North Sea is visible beyond sand dunes ahead. Cross the stile at the side of the gate across the path. A few yards beyond this there is a board (1) displaying information about Burnham Overy Staithe, part of Holkham National Nature Reserve.

The pines and sand dunes of Holkham Bay and, below, its mudflats and salt marshes.

The path continues ahead. Keep left at the fork, following the fence and hedge. Through the next gate the path continues along an embankment with reclaimed farmland on either side. It then goes through another gate and joins the Peddars Way and Norfolk Coastal Path. The embankment here is part of the sea defences, with the farmland on the right, lower than the coastal mudflats in places. There is a fine view over the bay from the elevated path. Turn right at the junction (2). Wet meadows and reed beds lie on the right – to the left are mudflats and saltmarshes, colourful in summer with sea lavender and other flowers.

The path rises and meanders among the dunes. At low tide it is easier to walk along the sandy beach, at other times continue among the dunes. There is no obvious path here, so head towards the wood ahead to the right. Just before coming parallel with the wood (3), turn right and head inland, climbing steeply up the dunes. From the top there is a spectacular view across the dunes, beach and sea.

Enter the pine wood, heading right towards the south. The path emerges from the trees and curves left, skirting the south edge of the wood, then passes among conifers again. At the crossroads (4) turn right and leave the wood. Ahead, a church tower is visible over the trees and, to the left of it is the top of a tall monument. The path turns left, following a water-filled ditch on the right, then passes through a gateway. There are wet meadows on either side, with pools and reed beds.

Leaving the nature reserve, turn right at the crossroads (5). The path turns sharp left towards the road. Climb over the gate, turn right and walk along the verge back to the car park.

History and Wildlife

THE north Norfolk coast between Hunstanton and Weybourne has extended outwards a mile or so in historical times, and is still doing so. Silt from out flowing rivers is deposited at sea and has constructed extensive saltmarshes and mudflats. A map of the area shows just how unstable this coastline is for it shows narrow spits of land reaching out into the sea, made up of deposits from rivers carved by currents.

This coastline was once a rich and busy trading region but now it is a

19

popular and peaceful holiday area. After the Norman conquest the coastal towns became busy ports exporting wool to Flanders. The wealth accumulated by the wool merchants was used to build grand houses and castles, and to build the interesting 'wool' churches, many of which remain today throughout the region. Now the old ports are land locked, their rivers and harbours mostly silted up.

Much of the marshland of this shore has been reclaimed for agriculture but large areas have been preserved and they are rich in bird and plant life. There are several nature reserves owned and managed by various conservation bodies. Although this area is growing outwards, it is prone to flooding and extensive sea defences, including dunes and embankments, have been constructed to counteract this threat.

Holkham National Nature Reserve was established in the late 1960s and its 10,000 acres are managed by English Nature in cooperation with the Holkham estate. Its saltmarshes, mudflats and sand dunes are internationally important habitats for a variety of coastal wildlife. The reserve, which is popular with bird watchers, has seen a considerable increase in breeding birds and wintering wildfowl over the last decade. These include little grebe, coot, lapwing, redshank, and several types of geese. The exposed mud at low tide is a rich feeding ground for waders.

Little grebe in winter plumage.

This part of the coast is renowned for its summer display of saltmarsh plants, which have to cope with occasional high tides. Purple sea lavender is dominant, intermingled with sea aster and samphire. The sand dunes support a variety of wildflowers among the marram grass, including ragwort, sedum acre, sea holly, thrift, sea rocket and salsola. Sand dune plants, with their extensive root systems and ability to survive occasional burying of their top

Sea holly.

20

growth, are vital in establishing this part of the shoreline which otherwise would be eroded by tides and wind.

The pine belt was planted to protect the sandy soil from erosion by wind. The roots of the trees bind the sand and resin from shed needles sticks the soil particles together. Deciduous trees, mainly silver birch, have colonised some of the more sheltered parts of the wood.

The extensive wet meadows and grazing marshes, with their pools, ditches and reed beds, are also important habitats, supporting wetland vegetation and its dependent creatures. The area immediately to the landward side of the pine wood is sheltered from the salty north winds and in consequence is particularly lush.

Places of Interest

HOLKHAM HALL, just south of the nature reserve, is the home of the Earl of Leicester. The Palladian style house designed by William Kent in 1734 for the 1st Earl has an entrance hall measuring 46ft by 70ft and 43ft high with a splendid staircase flanked by columns of pink marble. Its state rooms are filled with fine furniture of the period and house an impressive art collection which includes works by Leonardo da Vinci, Raphael, Rubens, Van Dyke and Gainsborough. The house, which is open to the public, stands in a park that covers five square miles and was landscaped by 'Capability' Brown in 1762. It has a a mile-long lake and a resident herd of deer.

The peaceful resort of Wells-next-the-Sea, two miles to the east, used to be an important port but now its beach is over a mile inland, due to silting up of the coastline. The former harbour is now a boating lake with the picturesque name of Abraham's Bosom. Huge eighteenth and nineteenth century warehouses loom over the waterfront road. Wells has some excellent fish restaurants overlooking the still active quay where whelk and shrimp boats land their catches.

Walk 3 ROMAN CAMP AND BEESTON REGIS HEATH

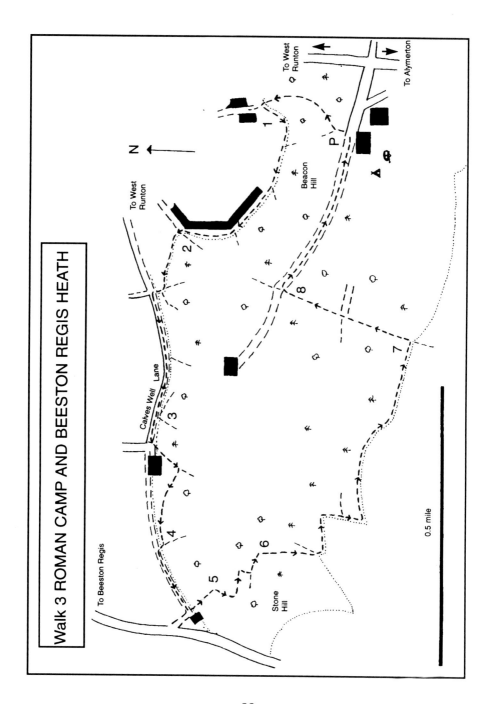

Walk 3

ROMAN CAMP AND BEESTON REGIS HEATH

Distance Three and a half miles

Map OS Landranger 133

Start/Parking Roman Camp car park; grid ref. TG184414. There is a small charge for parking. National Trust members free.

Nearest towns Cromer and Sheringham

ANYONE who believes that Norfolk is flat has not visited the area south of Cromer and Sheringham on the north coast. The undulating Cromer-Holt Ridge, clothed with woodland, scrub and heath, is undeniably one of the most beautiful parts of the county. The National Trust owns 167 acres just south of West Runton. The eastern end of the site is known locally as Roman Camp, although there is no evidence of Roman occupation. The western end is Beeston Regis Heath.

This short walk is mostly through woodland on the National Trust property and the area immediately to the south. There are open areas of heath, including Stone Hill at the western point with marvellous vistas over sea and countryside. Be prepared for some climbing up and down fairly steep paths. This is a perfect place for children as they can explore safely and freely the network of paths in the woods and clearings. Trails are generally good and well drained. There are several seats around the site, most with views. An information leaflet may be purchased in the car park.

Route directions

HEAD towards the flagpole. This vantage point, with seats, overlooks

West Runton and the North Sea. Take the narrow path on the right into the wood. There is a variety of attractive trees here including oak, beech and sweet chestnut with an understorey of holly and bramble. The path, which in places is not obvious, descends quite steeply.

The main path continues downhill, but take the narrow path to the left (1) – if you reach the wire fence on the left you have gone too far. The path curves right, following a wire fence on the right. There is a good view of the sea to the right.

Keep following the boundary for some distance. A bridleway joins the path from the left but continue ahead for about twenty yards. A wide path on the right leads to West Runton, but take the left path. There is a seat in a clearing (2) further up the hillside on the right. On reaching a junction of several trails, turn right, then left on to Calves Well Lane bridleway. Beyond the open fields on the right a curious coastal hill called Beeston Bump is visible. There is another clearing with a seat on the left.

The view from Roman Camp to West Runton and the North Sea.

24

At the signpost (**3**) continue ahead then, at the bungalow, turn left on to the narrow path by another signpost. Fork right at the next marker post. On reaching a bridleway crossing the path (**4**), turn right then immediately left on to Calves Well Lane again. Turn sharp left just before the houses ahead and climb up to the seat (**5**) on top of Stone Hill. This open heathland overlooks Beeston Regis, Sheringham and the sea, and is a fine spot for a picnic.

Take the path leading away from the coast. Fork left and walk parallel to the coast on your left, then go right and enter the wood. Turn left at the fence on to the bridleway, keeping the wire fence on the right.

Birds' nests in a silver birch.

At the junction with a wider path (**6**) an arrow on a tree points to Norfolk Heritage Coast. Turn right still following the fence then turn left at the end, keeping just inside the wood, then right along an avenue with a conifer wood on the left. The path turns at the corner and follows the edge of the wood, parallel to the road. Ignoring the paths on the left, continue until the path makes a sharp left turn (**7**). Here a sign to the right marks a footpath across a field. Take the path left into the wood. This straight track passes between mixed woodland. Continue ahead at the crossroads. Just beyond the fence with a yellow marker arrow (**8**) the path meets a dirt road with a stone pillar on the other side. Turn right along this road, which leads back to the car park.

History and Wildlife

The soil and rocks of this region are not native to Norfolk, but were carried here by glaciers during the last Ice Age. When the ice melted, it left

25

Bracket fungi on a silver birch at Roman Camp.

a series of moraines containing rock fragments from Norway as well as sand, chalk and flints from nearer parts. Large animal fossils are contained in the rocks of this area and many have been excavated from the cliffs between Sheringham and Cromer.

There are many historical remains in this area. In the woods at the west end of Beeston Regis Heath are numerous shallow pits dating from medieval times. They were used for smelting of the local iron ore, and slag from this activity may still be found in some of them. Beacon Hill towards the east of the site was, as its name implies, a look-out and warning point for invaders from the sea.

The heathland was formed by clearing the woodland for sheep grazing in earlier centuries. A large rabbit population also helped keep the heath clear of scrub and the area became colonised by heather and bracken and the grazing helped many wildflowers to flourish.

As in so many places, after the early decades of this century, grazing mostly ceased and the rabbit population was greatly reduced by myxomatosis. This allowed scrub and then woodland trees to invade this rare heathland. In 1992 the National Trust, with help from the Countryside Commission in a Countryside Stewardship Scheme, began work to restore and improve the heath. Major work has been carried out to join two of the remaining areas of heather into one large one, and to clear some of the encroaching silver birch. In 1993, paths and nature trails were marked out. This work received grant aid from the Norfolk County Council and three years later the scheme received an Environment Award from North Norfolk District Council.

The woods consists of a variety of trees, including sweet chestnut, beech, several species of oak, Scots pine, holly, rowan and silver birch. In the autumn an interesting variety of fungi appears on dead and living trees and

Silver birch

27

Grayling butterfly

The Gatekeeper

among the leaf litter. Heathland flowers, including bell heather, ling and foxgloves, abound in clearings and along woodland edges. Stone Hill is colonised by low scrub, mainly honeysuckle, wild roses and bramble and these fill the air with scent in summer. Many birds inhabit the woods, including wood warbler, green woodpecker, greater and lesser spotted woodpeckers, and tree pipit. Adders, lizards and slow worms may be spotted among the heather on warm days. Frogs and toads stay in the damper areas.

There are many butterflies in the heath and woods, among them the Purple Hairstreak, which has a fondness for the tree tops; the Holly Blue; the Grayling; and Gatekeeper. The site is managed by a group of local volunteers, who also raise funds towards its upkeep.

Places of Interest

HEAVY horses can be seen working at the Norfolk Shire Horse Centre near West Runton and also on display are various breeds of native ponies, some with foals. A barn is used as an indoor display area and here there are film shows and a display of photographs of horse drawn machinery, waggons and carts.

The Victorian resort of Cromer was once a small fishing village, but expanded when railways made the seaside more accessible. The old town is centred around an imposing Perpendicular church with its high square tower which was used as a lighthouse before the construction of a purpose-built one to the east of the town. Cromer is famous for its crabs which are caught from small boats launched directly from the beach. It has a fine sea front with a pier, a maze of narrow streets with shops, several parks and gardens, and a small museum.

Sheringham is another start-of-the-railway-age resort. The North Norfolk Railway is based at Sheringham station and trips can be taken on steam trains through attractive countryside to the market town of Holt five and a half miles away. This service is run by volunteers.

A few miles west, at Weybourne, is the Muckleburgh Collection of tanks, armoured cars and other military vehicles. Displays and demonstrations are held through most of the year and there is a licensed restaurant, picnic area and gift shop.

Felbrigg Hall, one of the finest seventeeth century houses in Norfolk, was left to the National Trust by R W Hetton Cremer, an authority on the county in that period. Among the books he wrote is *Felbrigg*, which traces the history of the house and the generations of the Windham family who lived there. The hall is set in extensive gardens and parkland two miles south of Cromer and has a library containing books formerly owned by Dr Johnson; a room full of pictures brought back from the Grand Tour by William Windham; and a drawing room with a wonderful plaster ceiling.

Walk 4 LITCHAM COMMON

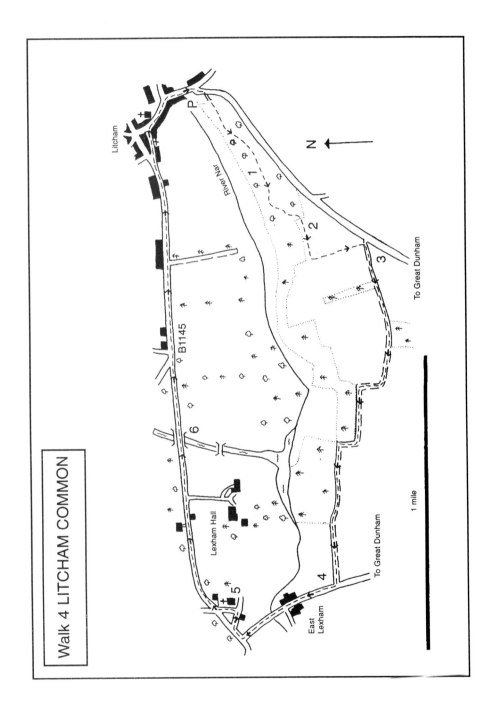

Litcham

River Nar

P

1

2

3

To Great Dunham

N

B1145

6

Lexham Hall

4

5

East
Lexham

To Great Dunham

1 mile

Walk 4

LITCHAM COMMON AND THE NAR VALLEY

Distance   Five and a half miles

Map   OS Landranger 132

Start/Parking   Car park at the east end of Litcham Common; grid ref. TF887173

Nearest town   Litcham

THE first part of this walk is through the Nature Reserve – the sixty acres of heath, wood, scrub and small ponds that straddle the Litcham to Great Dunham road. It is worth taking time to explore this gem more fully and further information about it can be obtained from Norfolk County Council. The path then joins the Nar Valley Walk and back-tracks to Litcham along a leafy lane that affords fine views of the extensive grounds of Lexham Hall.

Paths are generally good, except for one stretch of the Nar Valley Walk which is overgrown. The nature reserve trails may be muddy at times. Dogs should be kept under close control in Litcham Common Nature Reserve.

Route directions

FROM the car park take the grass path by the information board. This enters open deciduous woodland, mainly oak and birch with little under-storey. The trail is not very obvious in places but leads straight ahead. Some dead trees have been left and are host to some interesting fungi. Tangled branches of old honeysuckle are climbing some of the trees.

Fork left and take the wider trail which leads into a grassy clearing with meadow flowers (**1**). The main path continues along the left boundary of the clearing, through trees to another clearing and finally back into woodland. Several nest boxes have been attached to the trees in this dense birch wood.

Keep straight on until you reach a row of ancient oaks on the right, probably the remains of an old hedge. Just past these, at the junction (**2**) turn right and leave the nature reserve. Follow the marker posts on the Nar Valley Walk along the field edge. At the corner of the field, with its marker post, the path turns left along a low embankment and here it is narrow and overgrown.

On reaching the corner, head towards the gate (**3**) and take the wide track to the right which passes conifer plantations, first on the right, then the left. Continue to follow the track as it bends first right, then left, skirting the wood on the right. Lexham Hall can be seen through a gap between the trees and on leaving the woodland edge there is a fine view over the Nar Valley.

At the road (**4**) turn right onto the lane that slopes down towards East

Lexham. On the green is a most unusual – and a most usefully arranged village sign, pictured left. The name of the village is mounted on a crown-capped pillar that rises from the centre of a circular seat and provides a backrest for the sitter.

Above it is an octagonal tiled roof supported by hefty un-trimmed tree trunks and topped by a weathervane. The structure offers a pleasant and sheltered place to sit and perhaps picnic.

The road crosses the river and continues uphill. Turn right at the junction and on the right there is an unusual church **(5)** with a Saxon round tower, and it is worth a slight diversion to take a closer look.

Continue along the quiet leafy lane towards Litcham and soon the extensive grounds of Lexham Hall will appear on the right and the house itself will be partly visible behind trees. A bridge **(6)** crosses a curious artificial water course, now stagnant and silted, emerging from the river behind Lexham Hall.

At the next junction turn right and enter Litcham. Fork right, following the sign to Dereham, then right again. On leaving the village, take the road on the right leading back to the car park.

History and Wildlife

LITCHAM COMMON, formerly called South Common, was originally owned by the inhabitants of the forty two houses in Litcham. The Commoners were allowed to graze their cattle on it from Michaelmas to

The Church of St Andrew, just north of the village of East Lexham, has one of the oldest Saxon round towers in Britain.

33

Lady Day (March 25), after the grain crops had been harvested and it was also a centre of the village's social and sporting life. Litcham Cricket Club had a permanent pitch on the common from 1868 to 1906 and it was a favoured spot for fetes, fairs and flower shows. Other earlier activities have included cock fighting bull baiting and horse racing.

Since common grazing ceased, birch and oak have colonised the original heathland and in 1984 the common, the freehold of which is owned by Lexham Hall Estate, was declared a Local Nature Reserve by Norfolk County Council. Some areas have been cleared of trees to recreate the now rare heathland but continual work is needed to prevent these areas from returning to scrub.

Honeysuckle.

The reserve contains a variety of habitats, each with its own wildlife. There is woodland, wet heath, an old chippings dump, a traditional meadow grazed by sheep, acid grassland, and pools. The wet heath areas are particularly rare and valuable and support plants such as purple moor grass, ling, cross-leaved heath, woodrush, heath bedstraw and various sedges.

Many butterflies are found in the nature reserve, including the small Copper, the Gatekeeper, Tortoiseshell, Peacock, Ringlet and Skipper. Cinnabar moth caterpillars, illustrated left, feed on the ragwort growing on the chippings dump. The paths of the Nar Valley Walk are bordered in places with colourful wildflowers of chalk grassland, including hypericum, scabious, yarrow, chamomile, lesser bindweed, poppy and white campion. These areas are rich with bees and butterflies in the growing season.

The Holly Blue butterfly on a bramble flower.

Places of Interest

CASTLE ACRE, about six miles west of Litcham, is an aptly named village, lying mostly within the outer boundaries of a Norman castle, only the gatehouse and earthworks of which remain. There are also the impressive ruins of an eleventh century Cluniac priory with a Tudor gatehouse and walled herb garden.

The Norfolk Rural Life Museum and Union Farm at Beech House, Gressenhall, near East Dereham has, in the Union Workhouse of 1770, displays illustrating the history of the county over the past 200 years. There is a reconstructed village shop; saddlers, wheelwrights, and basket makers' workshops; and a farm labourer's home and garden.

Union Farm is a working farm of the 1920s. It has rare breeds of sheep, cattle, pigs and poultry; regular demonstrations of its Suffolk Punch horses at work; and a nature trail. The museum has a tea shop, picnic area, children's activities and gift shop.

Norfolk Herbs at Dillington, midway between East Dereham and Gressenhall, is a nursery with attractive gardens set in a conservation area.

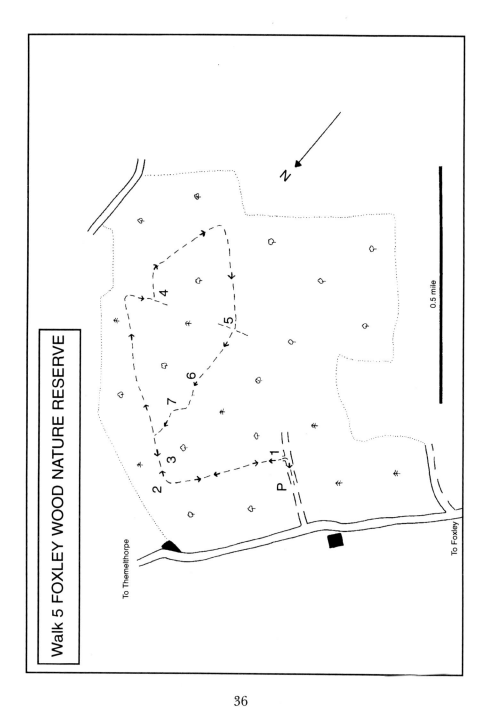

Walk 5 FOXLEY WOOD NATURE RESERVE

To Themelthorpe

To Foxley

0.5 mile

N

Walk 5

FOXLEY WOOD NATURE RESERVE

Distance   Three miles

Map   OS Landranger 133

Start/Parking Foxley Wood Nature Reserve car park just off the Foxley
to Themelthorpe road; grid ref. TG050229

Nearest town Reepham

FOXLEY WOOD is the largest remaining area of ancient woodland in
Norfolk, according to the Norfolk Wildlife Trust which owns and man-
ages it. This walk, although short, is full of hidden surprises. Among the
coppiced trees, trails and clearings, the walker suddenly comes across an
incredibly gnarled tree, a rustic seat or a piece of abstract sculpture.

The reserve is rich in woodland wildflowers which carpet the ground
in spring before the trees come into leaf. A sympathetic management
regime provides a number
of habitats to encourage
many varieties of birds,
insects and mammals to
live and breed here.

A special feature of
Foxley Wood is its network
of rides – the wide grassy
trails originally cleared to
assist timber transport but
now rich habitats in their
own right.

The wood is open daily

One of the network of rides in Foxley Wood.

37

except Thursdays. All paths are good but visitors are asked to keep to the marked trails, and keep well away from any heavy machinery when work is in progress. Dogs are not allowed in the nature reserve.

Route directions

FROM the car park, turn left along the wide track. This has broad margins which support a diversity of grasses, wildflowers and small trees and shrubs. The area is active with insects from spring to autumn, including various butterflies and large chirping grasshoppers. It is educational to contrast the regimented conifer plantation on the right with the natural mixed wood on the left. Several bird boxes are visible on trees in the reserve.

Turn left at the marker post (1) and enter the woodland. The oak standards in this area are around eighty years old, with a coppiced understorey, predominantly hazel with some ash. Turn right at the marker next to a seat (2). A few yards further on there is a giant flint sculpture (3) which looks for all the world like penknife piercing the ground. It is one of a

The 'penknife' sculpture and the 'fairy ring' of tree trunks.

38

Large scale coppicing has produced open, wildlife-rich clearings in Foxley Wood.

series of sculpture made in June 1991 from natural materials, mostly wood, by six commissioned artists – Lorna Green, Richard Bray, Christine Fox, Rosemary Terry, Bee Springwood and Dale Rowe. The purpose was to attract more visitors to Foxley, and this object was achieved that summer. However, most of those made of wood have now disappeared – returned to the forest from whence they came.

Continue ahead at the next junction. Birch and aspen dominate this area and several fallen trees have been left for wildlife and to let sunlight reach the ground. The path turns sharp right. After about two hundred yards, turn left at the junction **(4)**. The wood is dense here with many fallen trees. The trail emerges into the open and widens into a ride. At the four-way junction **(5)** take the track ahead to the right. Fork left at the marker post and take the wide path among the trees. Here, on the right **(6)** is another sculpture – a 'fairy ring' of tree stumps. A little fur-

The trunk of this birch trees bears the marks of the honeysuckle through which it grew as a sapling.

ther on, a gnarled old birch rivals in appearance the sculptures created by human hands. When it was a tiny sapling this tree spiralled up round a honeysuckle which left imprints on the trunk that grow ever larger.

At the next marker turn right. A few yards on there is a large open glade **(7)** on the right, obviously kept well mown to clear it of tree seedlings. The path veers left next to a bench and winds among birch trees. Turn left at the junction and retrace the first part of the trail past the first piece of sculpture and back to the car park.

History and Wildlife

FOXLEY WOOD was featured in the *Domesday* survey compiled for William I in 1086. It was mapped by the cartographer, Falen, in 1797 and appears to have changed little since then. For thousands of years it has been a valuable source of woodland products as well as a wildlife haven. Succeeding generations have harvested the wood as a renewable source of timber and there has been a periodic cutting back, or coppicing, of its hazel and lime understorey to provide wood for furniture, ship-building, tool handles and fuel. The thin flexible wands that sprout from a coppiced trunk, or stool, were woven into baskets and hurdles. Standard oaks provided beams for ships and house frames.

This century Foxley Wood was abandoned and became overgrown, with unpruned trees smothering the woodland floor. In the 1960s much of the wood was cleared and replaced with conifer plantations to provide timber for pit props.

When the Norfolk Wildlife Trust, (then the Norfolk Naturalists Trust) bought Foxley Wood in the 1980s it started at once to restore it to its former state with a traditional management regime, albeit using bandsaws and heavy machinery instead of axes. An intensive programme of renovation is opening up the wood again and encouraging wildlife. There is still a demand for coppiced products, including bark chippings for garden mulches, so a coppicing rotation of the understorey provides a commercially useful crop. The Trust estimates it will take more than 100 years to return the wood to its former state.

The oldest woods are the richest in species, and Foxley contains a vari-

41

ety of trees and shrubs, including oak, ash, hazel, birch, aspen and holly intermingled with Midland hawthorn, small-leaved lime and wild service tree. Some of the hazel and lime coppice stools are at least 500 years old.

It has a variety of soil types, so different trees and flowers grow in different areas. Hazel and oak predominate in some parts, while others contain birch and aspen with bramble and honeysuckle understorey. When an area is coppiced, sunlight reaches the ground and flowering plants flourish.

In spring and early summer, before the canopy is fully in leaf, the woodland floor is a mosaic of primroses, violets, dog's mercury, bugle, cuckoo flowers and wood avens. Some of the rides are seas of bluebells in April and May, and also support meadow flowers and an interesting variety of grasses and sedges. All these flowers provide nectar for butterflies such as the Meadow Brown, Comma, Orange Tip, the rare White Admiral, left, and the Speckled Wood.

The wood is a haven for birds, and nest boxes have been placed on some trees to encourage them. Goldfinch, sparrowhawk, and greater and lesser spotted woodpeckers breed here, and marsh, willow and long-tailed tits may be seen.

Weasel.

A number of mammals, including rabbits, hares, weasels, foxes and deer, live in the wood. A large clearing (7) once used as a woodcock shoot is now maintained as a sanctuary for nesting woodcocks and grazing deer.

Places of Interest

Two churches, and the ruined wall of a third, share the same churchyard in the eighteenth century town of Reepham. Hackford parish church was burnt down in 1543 and only a ruined wall remains, but the other

two, St Mary's and St Michael's, are still standing. The Old Brewery
House Hotel, built in 1728, has a sundial over the door.

The old station at Reepham is now a Museum of Shops, with exhibitions, a penny-in-the-slot amusement arcade, a gift shop and a tea shop.
Bicycles can be hired to ride along the former railway tracks and the
peaceful lanes as well as on the Children's Discovery ride or the adven-
turous Safari Ride.

Norfolk Wildlife Park at Great Witchingham, originally the private
zoo of naturalist Philip Wayre, was opened to the public in 1961. Its forty
acres of beautiful parkland contain a large selection of waterfowl and
European mammals, including reindeer, Barbary apes, wild boars and
bison. It is dedicated to the conservation of endangered species, and its
successful breeding programme has resulted in animals of some species
being returned to their natural habitats. There is a rabbit and guinea pig
village, a model farm with rare breeds, and the site is also home to the
Pheasant Trust, founded in 1959 to breed wild pheasants, now another
endangered species, and restock the natural populations.

About six miles from Foxley village, east along the A1067, the
Dinosaur Adventure Park at Lenwade is set in acres of wooded countryside. It contains a dinosaur trail, maze, adventure playground, crazy golf,
education centre, the Dinostore gift shop, a coffee shop and picnic area.

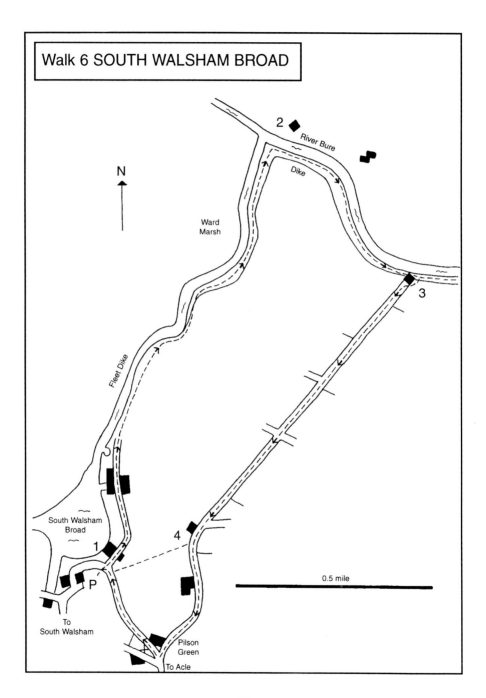

Walk 6 SOUTH WALSHAM BROAD

N

River Bure

Dike

Ward
Marsh

Fleet Dike

South Walsham
Broad

2

3

4

1

P

0.5 mile

To
South Walsham

Pilson
Green

To Acle

44

Walk 6

SOUTH WALSHAM BROAD

Distance   Four miles

Map   OS Landranger 134

Start/Parking The car park near the southeast bank of South
                  Walsham Broad, at the junction of Kingfisher Lane
                  and Fleet Lane; grid ref. TG372139

Nearest towns Acle, Horning

NO book on walks in Norfolk would be complete without a visit to
Broadland. This extensive region of waterways to the east of Norwich is
popular with tourists, yet is managed in a way that is sympathetic to
wildlife. Broadland is overseen by the Broads Authority which has won
an English Tourist Board's England for Excellence Award for its
approach to environmental tourism initiatives.

   There are numerous nature trails and conservation centres in
Broadland, but much of this walk is in one of the quieter, less frequented
parts. Some of the waterside paths are narrow and overgrown and can be
muddy in places.

Route directions

ON leaving the car park, turn left into Fleet Lane. The road soon reaches the little old church of St Mary and St Lawrence **(1)**, now converted
into a private garage. It is near the water side and on its wall is a plaque
showing it was built in 1786, and a barely readable map. Continue along
between boat yards and stores (there are public lavatories at the end of
the lane) and the road becomes a footpath and follows the right bank of
Fleet Dike. Marshes and meadows on the right, with drainage channels,

South Walsham Broad.

are grazed by farm animals. The path gradually narrows and becomes more overgrown, with a rich variety of wildflowers on either side.

After just over a mile, the Dike meets the River Bure and the path turns right to follow the river. On the opposite bank are the crumbling remains of St Benet's Abbey, **(2)** once a wealthy monastery whose monks were among the first people to drain the marshes and embank the rivers of Broadland. After the Dissolution a windmill, now also in ruins, was built within the walls of the abbey gate house. Every year, on the first Sunday in August, the Bishop of Norwich, who is also Abbot of St Benet's, travels by boat to hold an open-air service at the ruined abbey.

The river side path is built up to prevent flooding of the adjoining meadows, and gives a good view over the countryside. There are many old willows near the riverside, some more dead than alive. Just past the small brick building **(3)** where electric power lines cross the river, there is a small beach of piled flints – a suitable place for a picnic.

Near the building and between two willows there is a narrow bridge over a wide water-filled ditch. Cross this with care and turn right, under the power cables. The track curves left and continues straight, flanked by drainage ditches, their clean water supporting many aquatic plants.

This area is grazed by cattle, so watch where you tread.

Go around the gate across the path. The ditches here are lined with scented wildflowers in summer.

At Tiled Cottage (**4**) on the right, the track improves and curves left. (The public footpath over the stile on the right is a short cut back to the car park.) The main path becomes a road and soon reaches the outskirts of Pilson Green village. Continue ahead along this lane which has a species rich hedgerow on its right hand side. Turn right at the junction and continue along this road into the countryside and back to the car park on the left.

History and Wildlife

The Norfolk Broads are not natural lakes, but the flooded sites of peat excavations carried out by Anglo-Saxon and Danish settlers between 900-1300 AD. The Broads and their interconnecting rivers and dikes became important for commercial transport throughout the region, but now are noted for boating holidays, pleasure cruises and sailing.

Broadland is also attractive to nature lovers. Over the centuries a rich variety of plants and animals have colonised the lakes, dikes, rivers, reed beds and marshes. Unfortunately, since Victorian times, the once clear waters have become polluted in many places, mainly from agricultural fertilisers and sewage and oil from boats. This has encouraged the growth of algae which strangles larger water weeds and endangers many of the more delicate aquatic plants and the creatures that depend on them.

The work of conservation societies, amateur naturalists, the Broads Authority and Anglian **Dragonfly at rest on a rush.**

47

Water is invaluable in cleaning up and limiting the damage and ensuring that much of Broadland's wildlife survives. Now nature is recovering, and numbers of many species of rare plants and animals are increasing

South Walsham Broad is now one of the quieter broads, with some attractive old cottages on its southern shore. The tree-lined eastern part of the lake is privately owned.

The grazing marshes east of the broad and south of the river are typical of large areas of Broadland. Much of this land was reclaimed, first by digging drainage ditches, then by pumping water into the rivers. To stop flooding, embankments were built along the river banks. The recovered meadowland is used for grazing animals, and these marshes and ditches have themselves become important wildlife habitats. Grazing encourages wildflowers of damp meadows to flourish, while the margins and banks of the ditches support an incredible variety of scented and colourful flowers, including lady's bedstraw, valerian, thistles, great hairy willow herb, cow parsley and knapweed. Rare aquatics grow in the ditches themselves, including 'brandy bottle', yellow water lilies, aponogeton, water crowfoot and water violet.

Water mint and, below, water starwort

Places of Interest

SOUTH WALSHAM BROAD is the most eastern of a series of broads connected to the River Bure, with Wroxham Broad furthest west. There are several places in this region where boats can be hired, both self-drive and cruisers.In South Walsham, as at Reepham, churches share a churchyard. St Mary's and the remains of St Lawrence's were once in separate parishes, each with its own church and vicarage, but they combined around a century ago.

Fairhaven Gardens contain many rare plants and are especially attractive when the rhododendrons are in flower in early summer. There is a restaurant, gift shop and plant sales area. Boat trips are run from the gardens to St Benet's Abbey.

The Norfolk Wildlife Trust's Upton Fen nature reserve, with its exceptionally clean waters supporting a rich diversity of plants, is on the outskirts of South Walsham village, off the B1140 heading east. At nearby Ranworth Broad and Marshes there is a conservation centre and nature trail. Its wooden and thatched Conservation Centre is actually floating on the broad. There is a wooden trail suitable for wheelchair users.

The large village of Acle is worth a visit. In the opposite direction there is the yachting centre of Horning which has a ferry for foot passengers and cyclists crossing the river at the Ferry Inn.

St Benet's Abbey on the River Bure.

49

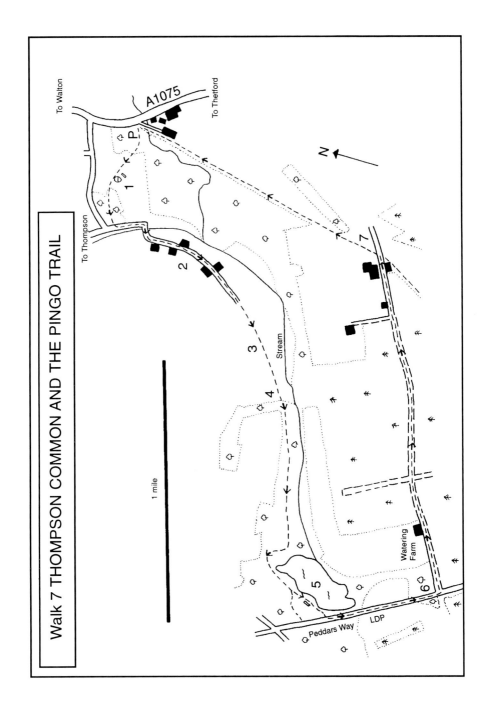

Walk 7 THOMPSON COMMON AND THE PINGO TRAIL

Walk 7

THOMPSON COMMON
AND THE PINGO TRAIL

Distance   Six miles

Map   OS Landranger 144

Start/Parking   The car park in the old railway yard just off the A1075 near Stow Beddon; grid ref. TL941966

Nearest town   Watton

THE entire Pingo Trail is some eight miles long, but this walk is a shortened version and includes part of the Peddars Way long distance path and a portion of the dismantled line of the Swaffham to Roudham Junction railway. Most of the walk is within the boundaries of Thompson Common, one of England's most important nature reserves. The footpath, which passes through a variety of scenery and habitats, is well marked and maintained and contains a number of stiles. Dogs are not allowed in the nature reserve.

Route directions

CLIMB over the stile next to the information board in the car park. The trail, well marked by posts with arrows, crosses a low bridge over a small stream and enters untidy deciduous woodland with holly and bramble understorey. Several shallow, circular ponds, the 'pingos' of the trail's name, are visible among the trees.

A second stile leads into a more open area of hawthorn and rose scrub. This is particularly attractive in early summer when the bushes are covered with flowers, and in autumn when the hips and haws begin to

51

The small lake (1) at the start of the walk and, below, the first bridge in the wood.

ripen. Follow the path for a short distance until you reach a small lake
(1). A wooden seat to the left is dedicated to the memory of Dr Charles
Petch, botanist and physician who, in association with E L Swann, wrote
the definitive *Flora of Norfolk,* published in 1963 by Jarrold and Sons.

Continue along the path, less obvious here, as it goes round the right-
hand side of the lake and cross over a stile on the left into deciduous
woodland. On reaching the lane ahead, turn left and walk past a few
houses (2). The road becomes a straight track, with undulating marshy
grassland to the left – occupied by a small herd of Shetland ponies, kept
to graze and help maintain a flower-rich meadow. Another stile (3) leads
into this meadow, which has a number of pingos. Follow the marker
posts carefully through the open area and climb over the next stile (4)
into the damp woodland of Thompson Carr. A bridge crosses a swift
stream, its clear water supporting several varieties of water plants.
Continue along the left bank of this stream. Old logs and tree trunks
have been left lying among the oaks and alders in this wood and have
become festooned with mosses and other plants.

Cross the iron and timber bridge on the right. Turn left at the marker
post on to a grass track, then fork left at the next marker. Thompson
Water (5), the largest lake in the Common, is visible through the trees to
the left. The main path skirts Thompson Water to the north and west,
but it is interesting to take a detour to the water's edge. A narrow trail
on the left leads to a clearing with a seat. This is a pleasant spot to take a
break and watch the water birds on the lake.

Follow this path along the bank for a short way, then turn right and go
through a gap in the fence to rejoin the main trail. Turn left on to
Peddars Way. Stanford battle area to the right of this track is itself an
important conservation site, the largest unofficial nature reserve in
Norfolk, with SSSI status. Its 17,000 acres, closed to the public, contain
evacuated villages, woods, and heathland grazed by sheep.

After about half a mile, turn left on to the bridle way sign posted to
Watering Farm (6). The Forestry Commission's Stow Heath conifer plantations along this bridleway are mostly hidden by attractive margins of
mixed woodland. Carry on past the farm buildings on the left and just

Evening at Thompson Water, an artificial lake created in 1865 and now an important waterfowl habitat.

after Crow Farm turn left on to the grass track by the sign which reads: 'Station Car Park – 1 mile' **(7)**. This final straight stretch of the walk follows the route of the old railway line through farmland, then woodland, before emerging by the station buildings back at the car park.

History and Wildlife

Thompson Common's woods, scrub and meadows are owned and managed by the Norfolk Wildlife Trust. They are dotted with the small circular ponds called pingos, relics of the last Ice Age and formed during the retreat of the ice sheet around 10,000 years ago. They were originally small hillocks pushed up when underground water froze and expanded. When the ice melted the hillocks collapsed into the space it had occupied and produced water-filled craters. The pingos were once part of a wide belt of pools which formed along the south edge of the ice sheet. Many of them have been lost to farmland, but the Thompson pingos have remained relatively undisturbed and have developed into rare and important wildlife habitats. They support aquatic plants such as bog bean, water violet and water bistort. Several dragonfly species breed in them, including the emerald damsel fly which was believed to be extinct until rediscovered at Thompson Common. Frogs, toads, newts and water beetles also live and breed in them.

Many centuries after the formation of the pingos, mankind moved in to the area. Peddars Way long distance path, probably built shortly after the Iceni revolt led by Boudicca in 61 AD, is one of the best preserved Roman roads in Norfolk.The name is medieval and means 'pathway'.

Stow Beddon station next to the car park operated from 1869 until 1965 when the line, known locally as the Crab and Winkle, was closed. Its busiest days were during and just after the Second World War, when it was used by servicemen at Watton Royal Air Force base. In its later years, Stow Bedon station regularly won prizes for best kept station but now the disused line is an important and relatively undisturbed wildlife corridor, rich in grassland plants and their dependent insects such as grasshoppers, bees, butterflies and moths.

Thompson Water is an artificial lake, created in 1845 by the damming of a small stream. Sluice gates near to the old ford site on the Peddars Way control its water level. Faden's *Map of Norfolk* of 1797 showed that this area of wood and water was previously heathland.

The larger pingos and Thompson Water are visited by wintering water fowl including coot, moorhen and various ducks. The reed swamps around the banks of Thompson Water, which has extensive mats of yellow 'brandy bottle' water lilies on its surface, are breeding sites for sedge and reed warblers, reed bunting, and many other species of water birds

Brandy bottle water lily.

The woods of the Pingo Trail support a wealth of wildflowers, including yellow iris, dog's mercury, marsh orchid and wood violet. Woodland animals include grass snakes and muntjac deer, as well as many birds. The reserve's damp meadows are rich in summer wildflowers such as marsh marigold, southern and early marsh orchids, greater spearwort and ragged robin. Butterflies abound in the meadows and old railway line, including the Brimstone, Holly Blue, and the White Admiral whose caterpillars feed on honeysuckle in the woods.

A reed bunting and, below, dog's mercury which is poisonous to humans and livestock.

Until around fifty years ago, grazing animals kept the meadows and the pingo borders clear of invading scrub, allowing wildflowers to flourish. However, since common grazing ceased scrub the trees have multiplied, endangering the grassland and pingos with their dependent wildlife.

The Great Eastern Pingo Trail was officially opened in 1989 and has been developed by Norfolk County Council with the Countryside Commission, the

Norfolk Wildlife Trust and the Manpower Services Commission. The Trust is currently undertaking urgent work to clear the encroaching scrub, hence restoring this internationally recognised site for the future. Ongoing management of the Pingo Trail is carried out by local volunteer groups.

Places of Interest

THE village of Thompson has an isolated fourteenth century church which is decorated throughout with intricate and beautiful carvings. Near it is the thatched Chequers Inn, also of fourteenth century date.

The market town of Watton is four miles north of Thompson Common. Just off the A1075, one mile south of Watton, is another important nature reserve, Wayland Wood. Parts of this small Norfolk Wildlife Trust site are believed to be a rare surviving remnant of the prehistoric wildwood which once covered much of Britain. Its most infamous claim to fame is that it is the setting for the Babes-in-the-Wood legend, thought to be based on true events.

At Great Ellingham, near Attleborough, are the Tropical Butterfly Gardens with hundreds of free-flying tropical butterflies and birds in landscaped gardens with pools and waterfalls.

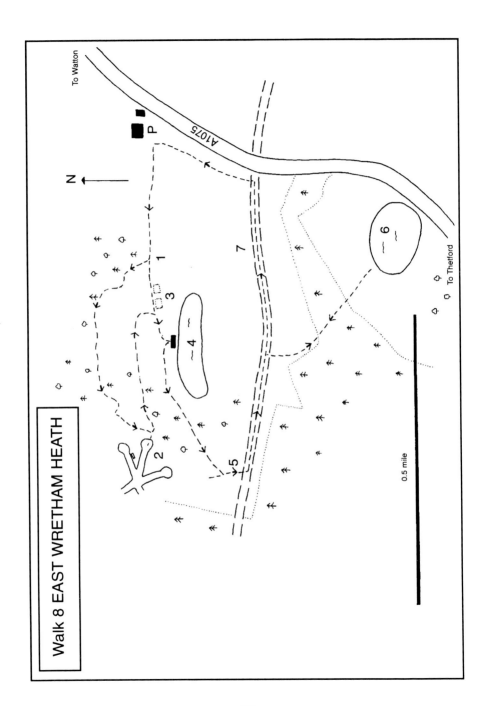

Walk 8 EAST WRETHAM HEATH

To Watton

P

A1075

To Thetford

N

0.5 mile

1
2
3
4
5
6
7

Walk 8

EAST WRETHAM HEATH

Distance   Three miles

Map   OS Landranger 144

Start/Parking   Car park at the warden's house off the A1075; grid
ref. TL912887

Nearest town   Thetford

A DERELICT wartime airfield and with overgrown runways and dispersal
points and airfield buildings hidden among the trees forms part of the
Norfolk Wildlife Trust's East Wretham Heath Nature Reserve in the
heart of Breckland. It makes a unique habitat for colonising plants and
animals and is fun to explore it. It is easy to get lost in the web of small
paths in part of the woods, but this does not matter at all because you
will soon get your bearings when you emerge into the open heathland.

There are some stiles on the walk and there are leaflets available at
the display board in the car park which include a useful map and details
of some shorter walks for those who do not want to do the whole trek.
An alternative trail for visually handicapped walkers is marked on the
board. The nature reserve is open daily from 8am to dusk.

Route directions

FROM the gate by the car park, go straight ahead along a wide grass
path among hawthorn scrub and open heath kept short by rabbits and
a flock of sheep. The sandy soil is riddled with rabbit warrens so watch
your step. Go over the stile (1) and fork right, following the green
arrows through the trees and clearings. The path twists and turns for
some distance and eventually reaches a concrete track. The path follows

the green arrow to the left, but it is interesting to detour to the right and investigate the crumbling panhandles of the old airfield dispersal points (**2**) with their colonising vegetation. Return to the original trail and continue following the green arrows. When the trail turns sharp right, ignore the arrow and continue ahead on the grass path. This soon reaches concrete and the remains of brick airfield buildings (**3**).

Now follow the white-arrowed trail to the right of the ruins and take the

next grass path to the left which skirts a fenced off area and eventually leads to the bird watchers' hide overlooking Langmere (**4**).

This shallow lake, which is fed by ground water, used to be a breeding ground for many varieties of water fowl but it has

Perhaps this building, surrounded by blast walls, was a bomb store when the the airfield was operational. Trees, plants and shrubs have taken it over.

been consistently dry for the last few years.

Return to the trail and continue to the left, following the white arrows. The mere bed is clearly visible over the low wooden fence to the left. The broad path weaves through pleasant woodland. At the T-junction, follow the arrow to the left and go through the gate. Still following the arrows, turn left on to Drove Road (**5**). A detour along the path to the right between two fenced off areas will take you to Ringmere (**6**), another dried up mere.

Continue along the lane. On the left is a memorial stone (**7**) to Dr Sydney Herbert Long, 1870-1939, founder of the Norfolk Naturalist

Trust, the precursor of the Norfolk Wildlife Trust, in 1926. Just before reaching the road, cross the stile on the left and follow the marker posts across the heath back to the warden's house and car park. There is a fine view ahead over the open countryside on this last part of the walk.

History and Wildlife

EAST WRETHAM HEATH was the first nature reserve to be established in Breckland, having been acquired by the NWT in 1938. For centuries the sandy heath had been grazed by sheep, cattle and rabbits, which prevented the land reverting to scrub. The rabbits were introduced to the area during the Middle Ages to be farmed for their fur and meat. Their descendants, together with a resident flock of sheep, are continuing to maintain the heath by keeping more vigorous plants, including bracken, at bay so that annual wildflowers and rare invertebrates, some of which are found virtually nowhere else in Britain, can thrive here.

This nature reserve was not always as peaceful as it is today. During

The memorial to Dr Syndey Long, founder of the Norfolk Naturalist Trust, now the Norfolk Wildlife Trust.

61

the war it was requisitioned and became part of East Wretham airfield, a satellite first of Honington, then Mildenhall.

From 1940 to 1945 Wellington and Lancaster bombers were based here and the Czech Training Unit also occupied the site. The military eventually left in 1970, and the crumbling remains of the wartime buildings and runways are now colonised by an amazing variety of mosses and lichens, as well as wildflowers such as wall pepper, vipers bugloss, wall bedstraw and dark mullein.

The heath grassland plants include wavy hair grass, harebells, thyme-leaved speedwell, spring vetch, early forget-me-not and heath bedstraw. This grassland supports rare spiders and moths, also many butterflies including Grayling, Essex, small Skipper and Brown Argus. Skylarks nest in the heath, and yellowhammers, goldfinches, tree pipits and willow warblers inhabit the hawthorn scrub.

Shelter belts of Waterloo pines, which have become wonderfully gnarled, were planted in the eighteenth century to consolidate the sandy soil endangered by over grazing.

Some oaks and birches have now colonised these plantations, and dead trees have been left standing to attract great spotted woodpeckers which eat wood boring insects. These small woods are now breeding sites for tawny owls, siskins and crossbills, and also are home for nightjars, moths and woodland butterflies. Heather grows in the grassy clearings beneath the pines.

The Waterloo pines, planted more than 200 years ago, nowadays present sculptured silhouettes to the Norfolk skyline.

The two pools, Langmere and Ringmere, have both been dry for the past few years as a result

62

of a large increase in the extraction of ground water. Their levels have always fluctuated, generally being higher in summer and low in winter, and they were important for breeding grebe and various ducks and wading birds. Now their dry beds are becoming colonised with vegetation.

Places of Interest

Thetford was the See of East Anglian bishops until 1091 and is full of fragments of religious foundations, the most substantial ruins being those of Thetford Priory, founded in 1104 by Roger Bigod for the Cluniac order and now owned by English Heritage and open to the public. The largely Elizabethan Bell Hotel has an extension overlooking the riverside promenade which leads to the Nuns' Bridges – a crossing point of the Icknield Way and the earliest trade route in England. Outside the King's House is a gilded statue of Thomas Paine, author of *The Rights of Man,* who was born in White Hart Street, Thetford in 1737.

Tawny owl.

The Charles Burrell Museum has a display of steam engines, agricultural machinery and reconstructed workshops dating from the eighteenth century.

South of Thetford there is another nature reserve, Barnham Cross Common, straddling the A134. This small reserve is bordered by the Little Ouse river and contains pine shelter belts, acid sandy heath and chalk grassland. It is managed by a local group of volunteers. To the west and north of Thetford stretch the Forestry Commision conifer plantations and sandy heaths of Breckland.

Walk 9 TIFFEY VALLEY, WYMONDHAM

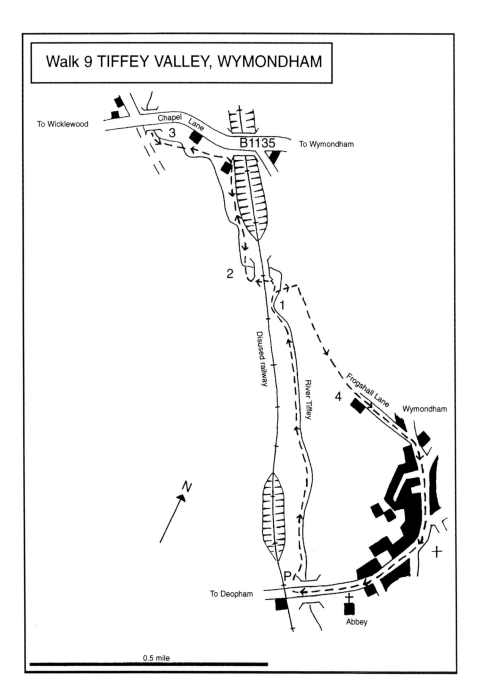

To Wicklewood

Chapel Lane

3

B1135

To Wymondham

2

1

Disused railway

River Tiffey

Frogshall Lane

4

Wymondham

N

P

To Deopham

Abbey

0.5 mile

64

Walk 9

TIFFEY VALLEY, WYMONDHAM

Distance   Three and a half miles

Map   OS Landranger 144

Start/Parking The car park by the river on Becketswell Road, Wymondham; grid ref. TG104014

Nearest town Wymondham

THE award winning conservation area on the outskirts of Wymondham, pronounced 'Windam', has only recently been restored to its original state after many years of cultivation. Fourteen of its eighty-one acres are now open to the public.

The path starts near the partly-ruined Wymondham Abbey and follows the River Tiffey for about a mile to Chapel Bridge, giving fine views over wetlands and water meadows. The trail then crosses a large meadow, grazed by sheep, on the other side of the river before returning to the car park via the narrow streets of historic Wymondham. This is an easy walk with good paths and seats at intervals. Dogs must be kept on leads.

Route directions

GO through the gate by the river. The road bridge here has two picturesque arches and a small waterfall. Follow the path along the bank of the swift and shallow river lined with trees and shrubs. Look back and you will see Wymondham Abbey behind the trees and shrubs of the river bank. The path soon becomes more open and the outskirts of Wymondham can be seen beyond the fields over the river on the right. An old railway signal towers over the trees ahead.

A profusion of wildflowers in a meadow grazed by sheep.

Ignore the footbridge **(1)** over the river and continue ahead for an 'out and return' to Chapel Bridge. Cross the disused railway line through the gates, then turn right and follow the railway, crossing the river at the bridge **(2)**. The river meanders through low lying meadows on the left. Fork left and cross the river again. Soon the path reaches a footbridge over a tributary stream next to Chapel Bridge **(3)** where there is a picnic table here under the trees. The river is wider at this spot, with fish, and is suitable for paddling.

Backtrack to the footbridge **(1)** and go over it into the field where there are usually sheep grazing. Continue ahead, then turn right along the path near the field boundary, keeping the ditch and hedge on the left. Cross the stile **(4)** and the path becomes a wider track, then a dirt road. At the junction, turn right into the outskirts of Wymondham. There are some very old timber and plaster buildings in this narrow street. At the war memorial, turn right into Vicar Street which leads back to the car park.

History and Wildlife

THIS conservation area was officially opened in November 1995, when it received a Norfolk Society award. Most of it was cultivated until recently, but patches of the original countryside remain. The landowners, with advice and help from the Countryside Commission and Norfolk County Council, have restored the waterside area and manage it traditionally with the aid of local volunteers. The riverside walk and part of the meadow are open to the public.

The Tiffey is a narrow river, little more than a stream, flowing swiftly in parts, widening to slow moving pools in others. Shoals of fish dwell in the clear water of the slower parts among the water weeds.

As well as the river, the area contains a mixture of habitats. Marshy grassland supports lush wetland plants such as butterbur, wild angelica, great hairy willow herb, purple loosestrife, meadowsweet, valerian, sedges and rushes. When in bloom in summer, these flowers attract clouds of butterflies, including the Meadow Brown, and other insects. The scrub and marsh plants provide seasonal feeding for finches, and the grassland attracts lapwings. Water shrews, kingfishers and dragonflies may be spotted along the river.

Along the banks, shrubs and trees provide shelter for birds and walkers. In places, dead and fallen trees have been left as yet more habitats for wildlife. Sheep are used to graze the meadows as part of the management regime, keeping the grasses short and allowing wildflowers to flourish.

Butterbur, so called because its leaves were used to wrap butter.

The walk is linked to a series of other open spaces, including the Lizard and Tolls Meadow, and forms a green corridor through Wymondham.

Water shrew in the reeds.

67

Wymondham Abbey and the River Tiffey.

Norfolk County Council plans to extend the walk further, eventually linking with Norwich.

Places of Interest

THE ancient town of Wymondham is centred on a market cross built in 1616 at a cost of £25 7s. It takes the form of an octagonal chamber raised on arcades and restored in 1989 for around £95,000 and is now the Tourist Information Centre. Wymondham Abbey was founded in 1107 by William d'Albini, Henry I's chief butler, and originally served the Benedictine monks and the people of Wymondham, an arrangement that led to all sorts of quarrels and disagreements. In 1249 the Pope himself intervened in an attempt to stop the bickering, but any success was short lived.

The abbey church of SS Mary and Thomas has two huge towers because of a fourteenth century falling out between town and tonsure. The monks built the present octagonal tower and put up a wall to seal themselves, and the high altar, off from the lay congregation. The townspeople retaliated by building for themselves the larger square west tower.

The Wymondham Heritage Museum is housed in the Brideswell, a former jail built in 1783 at the recommendation of prison reformer John Howard. It replaced the old Elizabethan prison described by Howard as 'one of the vilest in the country'. The building is now owned by the Wymondham Heritage Society and exhibitions showing the building's history as well as that of Wymondham and its industries are held there.

Walk 10 UNIVERSITY OF EAST ANGLIA AND YARE VALLEY

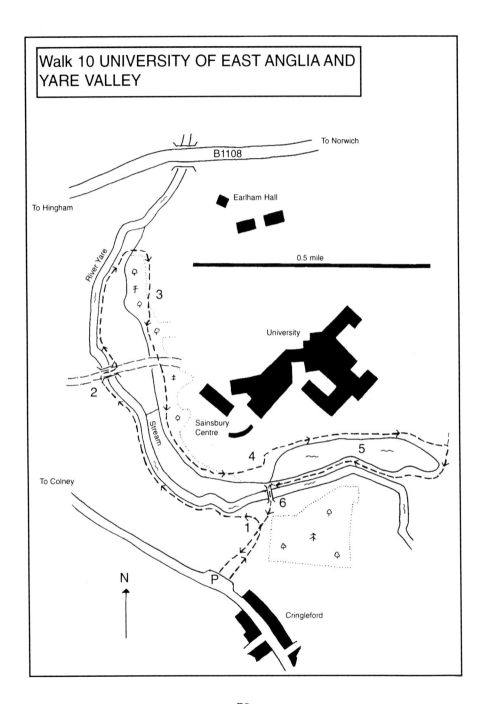

Walk 10

UNIVERSITY OF EAST ANGLIA AND THE YARE VALLEY

Distance   Three and a half miles

Map   OS Landranger 134

Start/Parking In the lay-by just north of Cringleford, on the
university side of the Cringleford to Colney road;
grid ref TG192067

Nearest town Norwich

THE campus grounds of the University of East Anglia, which are open to
the public, straddle the Yare valley and include an extensive and well
managed wildlife conservation area of woods, meadows and wetlands.
The most noticeable feature is the large artificial lake known as the
Broad.

It is interesting to compare this youthful reserve with ancient ones
such as Foxley Wood. It is also encouraging to see how quickly wildlife
colonises a sympathetically managed public parkland.

The walk passes through woods, along the river bank, and around the
Broad which is flanked by an extensive and beautiful summer meadow
on one side, and with wild wetland on the other. Dogs are allowed on
the campus but must be kept under control. The paths near the lake
and river can be muddy in places.

Route directions
Enter the university grounds through the small metal gate next to the
layby or, alternatively, through the wider barred gate towards the north

71

end of the layby, and take the left path among young mixed woodland; there are several branches and junctions but keep following the main path downhill. The university buildings can be glimpsed ahead through the trees. On reaching a wider track, continue ahead on the narrower path which soon curves left, and leave the university grounds through a gap in the fence next to a five-bared gate (1). Ahead can be seen the rugby pitch and buildings of the Institute of Food Research.

The path follows the left bank of the river Yare and reaches a road and concrete bridge (2). Cross the river here and go down the narrow steps on the left and continue following the river along its right bank. The water is quite deep but clear, with aquatic plants and fish visible. To the right is an extensive marshy meadow, rich in wetland wildflowers.

On reaching Earlham Park with its mown grass and benches, follow the woodland edge round to the right. Earlham Hall, built in the late seventeenth century, is visible higher up the valley side. The path eventually enters the wood (3). At the next junction, take the wider path lead-

Looking across the Broad to the strikingly modern university buildings.

72

ing right, then turn left after about twenty yards. The trail leads through a gap in the fence back into the university grounds. Cross the tarmac road ahead and continue into the wood. A water-filled ditch runs parallel to the path on the right, with the river beyond.

Fork right along the slightly wider path which shortly emerges into the butterfly meadow (4), a chalk grassland area dotted with small trees and shrubs. Take the left path across the centre of the meadow, then turn left along the wide track ahead. The Broad (5) is visible through the bushes on the right. Follow the path round the edge of the lake where there are several benches overlooking the water and the woods on the far side. Left of the path is a large wildflower meadow sloping up towards the campus buildings, including the futuristic Sainsbury Centre.

At the east end of the Broad go through the gap in the hedge and turn right along the track. This leads to the wild and marshy south side of the lake, with reed beds and wetland wildflowers; a detour can be made along the board walk on the left to study these more closely.

Flower of the Burnet rose and, below, reeds of the waterside.

Continue round the lake, between lake and river. This area is lush with wildflowers in summer. Cross over the arched metal bridge (6) on the left, then continue uphill back to the lay-by.

History and Wildlife

The University of East Anglia was built in the mid 1960s on the former Earlham golf course but much of its conservation area is less than thirty years old. Despite

Dead trees left in the campus wood to attract wild life.

its youth, it has developed a rich diversity of wildlife occupying wetland, woodland and meadow habitats. The university ground staff follow a strict management regime for each habitat, taking into account the needs of its wildlife.

The Broad lake was formed from a deep gravel pit, completed in the late 1970s, which self-filled with ground water. This lake is much lower in phosphates and ammonium salts than is the nearby River Yare. It is colonised with freshwater molluscs and crayfish and has been stocked with fish. In summer the lakeside is colourful with flowers, including the spectacular pink spires of southern marsh orchid. Once there was an island in the Broad where common terns nested but this has eroded away. Colonisation of the lakeside by marsh plants was slow at first because of the steepness of the banks, but as the edges have worn down, reeds and rushes have moved in.

The Broad supports a variety of breeding and migratory birds, including several duck species, coots, great crested grebes, ospreys, little terns and ring billed gulls. Dragonflies are plentiful in summer around the lake and river.

The large sloping meadow north of the Broad used to be mown short all summer, but since 1981 it has been managed as a commercial hay meadow, uncut till mid summer. Flowers appeared naturally as soil fertility decreased with removal of the hay. This is now one of the best floral hay meadows in Norfolk and new species are still arriving. One of the most spectacular is the Norfolk or hoary mullein, with sulphur yellow spires growing up to five feet tall over rosettes of large hairy leaves.

The butterfly meadow was created from the chalky soil removed from the gravel pit. The grass and flowers in this sheltered area support large numbers of butterflies, including the rare Green Hairstreak which breeds here. One third of this meadow is mown each year to prevent it changing into woodland.

Dutch elm disease killed many trees in the woods and the resulting gaps in the canopy have allowed woodland flowers to flourish, and the spring bluebell display is exceptional. Some dead trees have been left to attract woodpeckers.

The marshlands by the river are colonised by reeds and wetland flowers, cut occasionally to keep them in hand. The clean water of the shallow ditches contains rare plants including fool's water cress, water plantain and water violet.

Places of Interest

The Sainsbury Centre for Visual Arts in the campus grounds houses the wide-ranging and internationally important Robert and Lisa Sainsbury Collection which was given to the university in 1973. In the superb new Crescent Wing by Sir Norman Foster and Partners, 700 paintings and sculptures by Picasso, Moore, Bacon and Giacometti are on permanent display alongside art from Africa, the Pacific and the Americas.

The building also contains the university's own Collection of Abstract and Constructivist Art and Design, which includes modern architectural models and furniture designs. A programme of temporary displays and events is organised, including family activities, on the first Sunday of each month. There are also restaurants and a gift shop. The Centre is accessible to wheelchair users and disabled parking is available at the main entrance.

The historic city of Norwich is a jumbled mix of ancient churches and other buildings with modern shops, restaurants and cinemas. Its slender spired cathedral has a magnificent interior and contains the oldest bishop's seat still in use in England. Norwich's square Norman castle, 900 years old, is set on a mound overlooking the centre. It houses the city museum and art gallery, and guided tours of the battlements and dungeons can be taken to discover some of the castle's dark secrets.

Norwich Aviation Museum, two miles outside the city near the airport on the A140 Cromer Road, has a fine collection of historic aircraft, engines and memorabilia. An indoor display commemorates the presence here of the American Eighth Army Air Force during the last war.

APPENDIX I

Nature Conservation Societies and Reserves

Broads Authority, 18 Colegate, Norwich, NR3 1BQ. 01603 610734
Countryside Commission, Eastern Regional Office, Ortona House, 110 Hills Road, Cambridge, CB2 1LQ.
English Nature, Norfolk Office, 60 Bracondale, Norwich, NR1 2BE. 01603 620558.
Holkham National Nature Reserve (English Nature), Holkham, Well-next-Sea; tel. 01328 711183.
National Trust Regional Office, Blickling Hall, Aylsham 01263 733741.
Norfolk County Council, County Hall, Martineau Lane, Norwich 01603 222222.
Norwich Fringe Countryside Project, 69 Bethel Street, Norwich, NR2 1NR 01603 765476. Organises walks and events in the countryside surrounding Norwich.
Norfolk Wildlife Trust (NWT), 72 Cathedral Close, Norwich, NR1 4DF 01603 625540.
Ranworth Conservation Centre, Ranworth 01603 270453.
Royal Society for the Protection of Birds (RSPB), East Anglia Office, Stalham House, 65 Thorpe Road, Norwich 01603 661662; fax. 660088.
Snettisham Nature Reserve, 13 Beach Road, Snettisham, King's Lynn, PE31 7RA 01485 542689. Open every day. Entrance free. Toilets. Access for disabled. Organised events throughout the year.

APPENDIX II

Places of Interest

Castle Acre Priory, Castle Acre. 01760 755394. Open daily, April to October, limited opening other times.

Castle Museum, Castle Hill, Norwich. 01603 223624 or 621154 (weekends)

Charles Burrell Museum, Minstergate, Thetford. 01842 752599. Open April to October, weekends and bank holidays.

Cromer Museum, Cromer. 01263 513543. Open all year.

Dinosaur Adventure Park, Weston Park, Lenwade, Norwich, 01603 870245. Open daily during summer; limited opening in autumn.

Fairhaven Garden Trust, School Road, South Walsham. 01603 270449. Open Tuesday to Sunday and Bank Holidays, Easter to September.

Felbrigg Hall, Felbrigg, near Cromer. 01263 837444. Open Saturday to Wednesday, April to October.

Ferry Inn, Horning. 01692 630259. Ferry for foot passengers and cyclists.

Holkham Hall, Holkham. 01328 710227. Open afternoons, Sunday to Thursday, June to September, and certain bank holidays.

Muckleburgh Collection, Weybourne, near Sheringham. 01263 588210. Open daily, February to November.

Norfolk and Suffolk Aviation Museum, The Street, Flixton, Suffolk 01986 896644.

Norfolk Rural Life Musem and Union Farm, Gressenhall, East Dereham. 01362 860563. Open daily April to October.

Norfolk Shire Horse Centre, West Runton. 01263 837339. Open Sunday to Friday, April to October; Saturdays in mid-season.

Norfolk Wildlife Park, Great Witchingham. 01603 872274. Open daily, April to October.

North Norfolk Railway, The Station, Sheringham. NR26 8RA 01263 822045. Open most days, March to December.

Norwich Aviation Museum, Old Norwich Road, Horsham St. Faith. 01603 625309.

Norwich Castle Museum, Norwich 01603 223624 or 621154. Open daily.

Tourist Information Centres

Cromer – Bus Station, Prince of Wales Road, Cromer. 01263 512497
Hunstanton – Town Hall, The Green, Hunstanton. 01485 532610
Norwich – The Guildhall, Gaol Hill, Norwich. 01603 666071.
Sheringham – Station Approach, Sheringham. 01263 824329.
Thetford – Ancient House Museum, 21 White Hart Street, Thetford.
01842 752599.
Watton – Clock Tower, High Street, Watton. 01953 882058.
Wells-next-the-Sea – Wells Centre, Staithe Street, Wells-next-the-Sea.
01328 710885.
Wymondham – Market Cross, Market Place, Wymondham. 01953 604721.